Between Two Lives

Entre Deux Vies

A Maureen,
Bonne lecture et merci!
Laetitia

For Mum

Finally, a published book! Not what we expected – by any stretch of the imagination, in so many ways! – but I am delighted, and I know you are too.

Your strength and resilience are astounding. These are the only reasons you are still here and able to read these words.

Crumps Barn Studio
Syde, Cheltenham GL53 9PN
www.crumpsbarnstudio.co.uk

Cover design by Lorna Gray
Illustrations by Ceya

Typeset in Adobe Garamond Pro

All our books are printed on responsibly sourced paper from a mixture of managed woodlands and recycled material. Printed in the UK by CMP, Poole.

ISBN 978-1-915067-63-0

Between Two Lives

Entre Deux Vies

Laetitia Devic

with illustrations by Ceya

Crumps Barn Studio

BELOVEDS

I look at him
And I imagine …

He is so sad
So scared
So lonely

His beloved wife in hospital
Both waiting for time to pass
Till visiting hours

Just as I am sad
And scared
And lonely

My beloved mum in hospital
Waiting for time to pass
Till visiting hours

Slowly eating his breakfast
He pushes crumbs around his plate
His eyes lost in space

Deep in thought
About his wife

He remembers her beauty when he first laid eyes on her
He pictures the last smile she gave him
As he left her in the big white bed last night

He longs to see her again today
When visiting hours resume
And to hold her hand once more

Reassure her
Be there for her

Be her spokesperson
Her nurse
Her best friend

Her doctor
Her lover
All at once

Suddenly a woman appears
Full of energy
A strong and assured voice
'Ça va, papa?'

He is not alone after all!
Not sad or lonely, silly me!
They are here to visit Paris
On a father-and-daughter trip!

I look at them
And now I imagine …

She took him to the top of the Eiffel Tower
To lunch in his favourite restaurant
They glided along the Seine on a *Bateau-Mouche*
And he surprised her with dinner near Notre-Dame

They walked up the Champs-Elysées
Sparkles in their eyes
Reflecting the twinkling lights
Sprinkled around the trees

They were like children at a fun fair
Remembering the sights and smells of her childhood
Reminiscing about his antics
When they went on such Parisian trips

'Ça va, mais tout cela m'inquiète …'

He is worried
About his wife
– her mother

I hear his muffled words
He thinks she only has a few days to live
I see tears in her eyes

I was right after all
He is here to be with his wife
In her last hours

No trip up the Eiffel Tower with his daughter
No floating down the Seine arm in arm
No exquisite food in elegant restaurants

It is pure sadness and angst
Reflecting my own
About my mother

We are on the same boat after all
He, his daughter and I
Anxious and riding the waves

The rollercoasters at a misery fair

Eiffel Tower

TWO ONLY DAUGHTERS

Two only daughters
One with a mother no longer
The other slowly losing hers
And becoming her own elder

In these hard times
Among white sheets
Yellow blankets
And blue gowns

She tends to her
She reassures her
She tells her she loves her
She is *with* her

And she remembers
All the mother figures
Who were present
Throughout her life

Her nannies and babysitters
Her grandmothers and childminders
Her 'second mummy'
Who just this year survived cancer

Between four white walls
Two only daughters
Two lonely daughters
Whose roles are now reversed

SPLIT

Split
Between two lives
Split
Between two countries

Even in Paris
I
Am
Split

Beautiful sites
In the morning
Harrowing sights
In the afternoon

The City
Of Lights
My mother
In hospital

Four hours of fun and beauty
Eight hours of fear and pain
Me time
Mum time

Hours of magic
Hours of agony
Times of wonder
Times of heartbreak

My brain is split
Taking in one experience
After another
Compartmentalising the hours

To make sense of the events
The contrasts
The splits
The shards

Then late into the evening
I am split again
When it is time to update
My friends and family

When I'm here
I'm there
And when I'm there
I'm here

I collapse into bed
And break down in tears
Unable to bear
The unpredictability of it all

Trains cancelled
Lines damaged
Strikes
Suicides

I come home and I don't know
Where I am
What language I'm speaking
Which words I'm supposed to use

I feel guilty when I enjoy Paris
I feel guilty when I enjoy my warm bed
In my new house
While my mum is alone in a hospital room

I can't win
I have to keep bobbing
On the waters of uncertainty
I have to keep going

Going back and forth between two countries
Sleeping in hotels
Dozing on hospital chairs
Resting on trains

Cosying up to my husband
Cuddling my children
Playing with my cat
Finishing unpacking our boxes

Holding my mum's hand
Taking pictures of the Eiffel Tower
Eating my mum's hospital dinner
Savouring meals in Parisian cafés

Contrast
Split
Frag
men
ta
tion
of
my
spirit

AT THE JARDIN DES PLANTES

She
Fiery hair
Deep orange and wavy
All the way down to her waist
Slender and tall
Light-blue jeans

He
Grey hair
Stray strands blowing
In the gentle breeze
Slim and even taller
Smart dark trousers

She
Leaning into him
Laughing, smiling
Talking incessantly
Her sparkly green eyes reaching for his gaze
Her arm tightly woven into his

Showing how much power she holds over him
Revealing how much she OWNS him

He
Proud

She
Half his age

Both so in love

NINE YEARS

Morning, dusk and dawn
Three meet-ups in 24 hours
After nine years since our last encounter
Making up for lost time

Our first hug in 468 weeks
So tight, so delicious
Lingering to make it last
In our hotel lobby

And yet it is as if we had never parted
How can time be so compressed?
Did we perhaps in fact see each other just last week?
Is it a time trick? A brain ploy?

Through emails and messages
In online meet-ups and phone calls
Our friendship has stayed strong
Despite our respective struggles

Picking up where we left off
4,717,440 minutes ago
Arm in arm
Off we go to the fifth *arrondissement*

Paris at Christmas
Brightly lit streets and dazzling shops
Two old friends
Ambling along the Boulevard Saint-Germain

From sweet stalls with Eiffel Tower lollipops
To a welcoming woman selling hand-made jewellery
We let Paris enchant us, broad smiles on our faces
Laughter echoing above the traffic

Rings and bracelets galore
Shiny stones and intricate designs
Shall we try?
Shall we buy?

Christmas presents for each other
Our fingers and wrists forever bonded
Through mesmerising adornments
Memories forged in an instant

Carrying on to Carrefour de l'Odéon
I have kept the best surprise till last
My favourite restaurant, Les Éditeurs
The perfect place for us both

Bookworms
Editors
Proofreaders
Authors

Book titles shared
Writing tips exchanged
Literature references mentioned
Writing sessions scheduled

It is our time to shine
Not just our fingers and wrists
In friendship as in authorship
Not a minute to lose

We will meet again
Soon
We will not wait
Another 468 weeks

We will write together and
Our books will be published
Our legacy set on paper
For ever

JUST ONE ROOM

Reminders on my desk
Can't forget a thing
Planned meals on the fridge magnet
Can't forget a thing

Everything is scheduled
Everything in its place
Everything under control
Before I go and lose it all

Long hiatus
What happens when I leave?
No time to think
No energy to worry

I hope everyone stays healthy
I pray I don't catch anything nasty
I hope I have remembered everything
I take four trains, I go go go

I arrive in my hotel room in Paris
And I realise …

This is why
I could cope
With my neurodivergence
In my twenties

One room
One town
One job
One friend

No confusion possible
Ease and peace
Calm and freedom
Sometimes boredom

But tranquillity all around me
(If not always in my mind and body)

I knew where everything was
No angst at not finding a specific object
No time wasted
Serenity

Now in my hotel room
This is what helps me cope

Some days I cry
Other days I feel overwhelmed
But my *one* room at least
Keeps my brain calm and organised

One suitcase whose contents fit into
One tiny wardrobe
One pair of shoes, three tops
One small computer

My life in a piece of luggage
My needs within arm's reach

I come back home after two weeks
It feels like everything is everywhere
Like my routine is out of the window
Like my life is spread around all rooms

Paperwork scattered throughout the house
Sticky notes in my study
Bills in the kitchen
Wads of paper in our bedroom

Reminders
Ideas
Tasks
Chores

Food in our fridges and freezers
Who knows what is where
What needs to be consumed first
(We've just moved, we're still working things out)

I don't remember where things are
I open the wrong cupboards
I tick off the wrong lists
I speak the wrong language

Lost lost lost
Panicked panicked panicked
So much to catch up with
So much to plan for my next trip to France

People to update
Phone calls to make
Appointments to honour
Presents to buy and wrap

My suitcase stays
In our bedroom
No point in putting it away
In the attic

Half emptied
Half loaded
With things I will need again
In just a few days

I may go crazy
I may fold under the weight
Of all these responsibilities
Here and there, there and here

Swinging from one country to the other
From one house to one room
From one room to one house
Like a pendulum over the Channel

In our new home
Simplified organisation
With boxes and trays
In cupboards and drawers

But it's not enough

Put me in a hotel room any day
Or in a studio like in my twenties
Give me back my peace and ease
Pretty please

St Pancras Station

FOUR WOMEN IN A TAXI

Train suddenly terminating at Reading
Just one stop away from London
What is happening?

The lines are damaged
You can wait
Or you can go

Mild panic in my heart
What to do?
I will miss my Eurostar
No matter what move I make

I find it hard to take decisions
But in times of crisis
They come easily to me
A taxi it will be!

A woman approaches
And asks me
'Would you like to share a taxi with me?'
Grand idea, even better! Let's share the cost!

When I return to her
After a loo stop
She has recruited
Two more women!

'St Pancras is perfect!'
Thank you Universe
How easily
You orchestrated the whole thing!

And how apt
That these two women
Are musicians
In an … orchestra!

I am in awe of how we came together
In the space of ten minutes
And how we all get on
Instantly striking a friendship

A black cab turns up
We all stack up
Onto the battered
Leather seats

Squeezing our legs
And our luggage
We all just fit

Four women in a taxi
For ninety minutes
Chit-chatting away about

Motherhood
Music
Poetry

Travel
Work
Children

As if we had known each other for decades
As if we took a taxi to London together
Every Sunday morning!

We laugh and we share
We talk and listen
We check our watches
Discuss our deadlines

I miss my Eurostar
But it was worth it
The most fun I've ever had
With total strangers

A welcome distraction
Just hours before seeing Mum again
After her fourth back operation
Which won't be the last

BETWEEN LIGHT AND DARKNESS

She moves between light and darkness
Endlessly
Day after day
Night after night
Her daughter faultlessly by her side
Providing comfort and soft hope

They laugh and they cry
They talk and remain silent
They sleep and they look outside
At the azure vault or the grey clouds
At the skyscrapers in the distance
Tall and immutable

The daughter feels like a medicine woman
Using all her skills to support her mother
Physically and emotionally
Mentally and spiritually

She is her life doula
Her nurse
Her physio
Her coach
Her therapist
Her scribe
Her secretary
Her anointing Priestess

All wrapped into one

As her mother drifts between light and darkness
Swaying between life and death
Has choice been taken away from her?

Some days they see the brightness
At the end of the tunnel
Other days only its dimness
Some days she sleeps and sleeps
Other days she talks and talks

Wandering down the corridors of morphine
She dreams
She hallucinates
She mumbles

She sits up
Thinks she is home
And wants to walk out

Her daughter watches
Tears in her eyes

When will this get better
Once and for all?

EXTENDED FAMILY

I had been fearing for a while
That I would be lonely and alone
Once Mum wasn't around any more

Who would care about me?
Who would care *for* me?
Who would support me

If anything went wrong
With my family
Here in England?

After all, we have been living
In relative autonomy and aloofness
Not involved in other people's lives

I shouldn't have worried

As soon as I created our virtual group
To keep people abreast of developments
In relation to Mum's operations

All our family
And her closest friends
Rallied around us

In such a tight way
That we could feel love and support
Through our devices

Words of comfort
So we would stay strong
Words of encouragement
So we would be brave

Words that made us smile
Words that made us cry
Words that made us laugh
Words that made us feel

That we would make it

Phone calls in tears
Anxious hearts
And heightened emotions

They were always there
A steady and
Rational presence

When I cried alone
In the middle of the night
I felt their strength and love
Even in their absence

The most precious gift
In these intense weeks
Was reconnecting
With my two cousins

Last time we had met
We were sixteen
And barely knew each other

We skipped thirty years
Reunited as fully grown women
Mothers of teens and young adults

We hardly talked about the past
And just picked up
Where we were in our lives

Their parents, aunt and uncle
Just as concerned and reassuring
A unique presence in those difficult times

My own paternal uncle and aunt
And their son and daughter, my other cousins
Equally supportive

So … I *do* have a family
A large family
One beyond my mother

It warms my heart
I feel relieved and happy
I will not be alone after all

I will still have bonds
With my country
And my extended French family

CHRISTMAS IN MALMESBURY

Mum is in good hands
Her cousins keep her company
I can spend Christmas in Malmesbury
With my husband and children

The Eurotunnel strike has shortened my stay
By 48 hours
I only have four days
To savour the festive season in our new town

The Old Bell Hotel
At its most elegant
With the dark red bow and golden bell
Above its door

The mesmerising baubles
Surrounding its threshold
The Christmas tree twinkling in the night
Beckoning us with its big bright star

The neighbouring Abbey
Majestic in its grounds
Historic and contemporary
A reliable presence

House roofs lined with fairy lights
Shops playing Christmas songs
Restaurants and cafés serving warming food
Turn Malmesbury into an enchanting town

I walk around in a daze
Wondering why we're here
And not in Wallingford
Our previous home of twenty years

But also enraptured by the atmosphere
Relieved to be with my family
Getting to know our new town together
With warmth in our hearts and all around us

Candles lit in windows of
Rows of tiny cottages right on the pavement
The town wants to be part of us
As we are part of her

An engaging community
Thriving on art, literature
Music and history
A welcoming borough

Thank you Caer Bladon
For making
Our first Christmas here
Truly magical

Malmesbury Abbey

TEAR

I never want to leave my babies
Every departure is a tear in my heart
Yet every single one of them is necessary

Then from the other side
Every departure is another tear in my heart
Not knowing if I'll ever see her again

Wondering in what state she will be
When I next see her
If I see her

Often asking myself if I will be safe
On my next journey
And will see my babies and darling again

The dance between those I love
Between my two countries
Continues

My heart shredded
Torn to pieces
Beyond recognition

LE SACRÉ-CŒUR

When I travel by Eurostar
I always spot it
Its white bulbous towers
Like a fairytale castle

When I see it in the distance
I know that we are in Paris
That we are close to our arrival at Gare du Nord
And it makes my heart swell

Today, I'm going to see it up close and personal

Synonym with breathtaking 180-degree views
of the City of Lights
Delicious *crêpes*
Painters and paintings
Music and photographs

Its white steps
Are stacked with tourists
Cameras around their necks
Phones in their hands

But I am not one of them

I am Parisian
And I *feel* Parisian
I join the artists
Admire their portraits and landscapes

And I remember …

1999
You lost your life in a tragic car accident
1998
The last time we saw each other

Your flat was just a stone's throw away from the Sacré-Cœur
So tiny but so perfect
We ambled along the cobbled streets
Watched the painters on Place du Tertre

Even toyed with the idea of having our portrait done

How I wish I had insisted!
I would have something recent of us
To smile at and remember you by

Rather than the photos of our childhood
Our cute small noses
And tiny bright eyes

We were nearly twins
Born eight days apart
And were inseparable

Aside from patchy memories and those images
All I have is a black-and-white photograph
Of you, smart in your dark suit

I don't even know where you were going
Or where you had been
But you looked happy

You always knew you would die young
I don't know how or why
But for me

Le Sacré-Cœur will always be
The symbol of our last day together
So special in the darkest place of my sacred heart

Le Sacré-Cœur,

THE SEASON OF THE *GALETTE*

At freezing Gare de Lyon Station
Is my favourite *boulangerie*
It's the season of the *galette*
The delicious *galette des rois*

Its soft yet crumbly almond paste
Between two sheets of puffed-up dough
Golden, fluffy, crimped, delicate
Its secret hid in the middle

Who will be king?
Who will be queen?
Who'll wear the crown?

A beggar hangs around for coins
I think I'll get him a *galette*
To help him silence his hunger
And celebrate the brand-new year

I ask for two lovely *galettes*
One for him, one for me, hungry
'It's three for two', the baker says
What a treat, Mum will get one too!

I turn around and see he's gone

Out of the station fast I walk
Another beggar comes to me
'Some coins, or a fag, or some food?'
I offer him my spare *galette*

With a twinkle in his brown eyes
He asks if it's an almond one
'Yes,' I say, 'take it, here here,
Wishing you a Happy New Year!'

'It is cold, thank you', shivering
'It really is, I'm so sorry'
'Merci madame, merci', bowing
And we part ways, *galettes* in hand

PARALLEL WORLD

I live in a parallel world
In and out of England
In and out of France
In a strange bubble

A bubble that doesn't belong to me, or our family
Or our house
Or my mum
Or her life

A bubble outside of time
Outside of space

I'm mostly in it
But sometimes have to come out of it
To face the reality of the 'Other World'

It's a bubble I've put around me
But it's also one that decided to envelop me
Of its own accord, in order to protect me

As I travel
I leave pieces of me along train tracks
In train stations
On carriage seats

Along corridors, pavements and roads
In hotel rooms
Cafés and restaurants

Chunks of my brain
Shards of my energy
Scattered all over
England, the Channel and France

Sometimes I don't know where I am
I don't know which language to use
I get the wrong words out
In the wrong tongue

My family in England
Doesn't really know what I have been through
My mum in France
Doesn't really know about my life 'in between visits'

I live in a parallel world
Incomprehensible to all of them
Inconceivable to me

ON THE EUROSTAR

On the Eurostar
On Imbolc
Another journey
Another transformation

I have hyperacusis
I can hear everything they say
At the other end of the carriage
It echoes strangely in here

The munching sounds
The dialogues
The laughter

The coughing
The click-clacking of someone's keyboard
The words spoken down a mobile phone

Still, my mind drifts
Half awake
Half asleep

Then everything gets dark
We are under the Channel
In between countries
Dim lights dotting the tunnel

At what point do I become French again?

When we emerge out of the tunnel onto Froggyland?
When I arrive at my mum's three hours later?
When I start speaking French –

Whether that's on the train
In Paris
Or in my childhood home?

Or am I *always* French, really?
It's just that to *me* my Frenchness is dormant
Buried deep within
Only showing up when I let my guard down …

Or is it all completely subjective?
Everyone in England sees me as French
Everyone in France sees me as French
It's only me who chooses what to be?

Sometimes confused
When I shouldn't be?

My Frenchness
For everyone to see, hear and sense
But hidden from *me*
Only revealed once in a while?

Yet there is only *one* me

I arrive and I feel totally French
Un-confused
With a spring in my step
And lightness in my heart

Paris is my home
The City of Lights
Where I was born
My forever love

If I don't go there for a few months
I start missing it

I feel itchy to return
My heart whines and cries
I have visions of Notre-Dame
And my favourite restaurants

That's when I know it is time
To go back
But today
It was not my choice …

I WANTED TO GO BACK TO PARIS MORE OFTEN

I wanted to go back to Paris more often
But not *that* often

Be careful what you wish for

I forgot to specify how often
And why …

Eight times in five months
That was *not* the plan

Five operations in one month
That was *not* the plan

Thanks for listening, Universe
Next time, I will be more specific

A BRAND-NEW LIFE?

Five operations in her back
Two stents in her heart

A new back
A new heart
A new lease of life?

Heart flutters
Wooziness
Unsteady on her feet
And now out of breath

A new lung too?

Will she ever recover
And have a brand-new life?
Or is this a very slow

And painful end?

Notre-Dame

NOTRE-DAME

She rises
Her two towers overlooking the river
Keeping an eye on its boats
And on the never-ending tourists at her feet

She witnessed my birth
From across the road
– yes, I started life at the Hôtel-Dieu
The oldest French hospital

Notre-Dame holds a special place in my heart
I always photograph her
Even though I already have hundreds of pictures
Of her towers and portals

I love walking around her gardens
In the spring and summer
Smelling her roses
And her cherry blossoms

I was devastated when so much of her burnt down
I couldn't watch the news
Too scared of what I would see
– or would *not* see …

Today is the first time
I have looked at her since her fire
She seems sad
And naked still

I only photograph her from the front
Even though there are temporary buildings
Cranes and other unsightly machines
On her parvis and near her sides

Even though I can see
The scaffolding around her middle
And at her back
From all angles

As I polished this poem
I watched the footage of her fire
For the first time
And I shed a few tears

The black holes
Unfathomable
The work to repair her
Seemingly endless

It has been five years
I hope they will soon be done
I want her restored to her former glory
My dear Notre-Dame

Afterword

As I complete these lines
The works are finished!
She is dazzling
Like a diamond in the city!

Thank you
All firefighters who rescued her
All philanthropists who gave money
All experts who built her back up

For us all to enjoy
Notre-Dame
Once more
Restored, renewed

Victor Hugo is happy
In his tomb at the Panthéon
This chapter can be closed
But the book lives on

THE SINGER AT LES HALLES

I am sitting on a stone bench
In the first bit of sunshine seen in 11 days
The bright star finally out from behind the clouds
After days of grey and rain

A man is sitting across from me, in the distance
Old French songs
New African ballads
The sounds of his guitar echo in the large square
of Les Halles

There is magic and softness in the air
Languidness and slowness
As the guitar man plays 'Le Pénitencier'
His words carried by the breeze

The majestic golden waves of Les Halles
In the heart of Paris
Welcome all visitors in their belly
A whale in the centre of the French capital
Housing hundreds of shops, cafés and restaurants

Mixing English, French and an African tongue
The man's songs reflect the international presence
In the new-look *ventre de Paris*
(Would Zola recognise it?)

Where just a couple of centuries ago
There were only fruit, vegetable, meat and fish stalls
 and Parisians
Prices and names shouted under glass vaults
Today there are brightly lit shops and people from
 around the world

Behind me, Saint-Eustache gleams against the blue sky
Its light, cream-coloured stone freshly restored
Should I go in?
No time

In any case, I cannot move, hypnotised
The guitar and the deep voice still enthral me
The repetitive rhythms and rhymes of the guitar man
Are like a lullaby

Eyelids and cheeks kissed by the warm rays of the sun
I feel sleepy in the tender afternoon
I could stay till dusk and beyond
Here in the enchanting belly of Paris

But London beckons
My Parisian parenthesis is over

Time to go home
Time to board the Eurostar again
Time to doze on the train
In the darkness of the night and the tunnel

Then it will be time to walk to the Tube station
And ride the Underground to Paddington
Then take yet another train
To Swindon, and then the car home

It is exhausting
A few days in England
Double the time in France
But I do my best to find joy in most moments

Even in intensive care
The joy of seeing Mum
Making small progress
Every day

Even if it is three steps forward
Two steps back
Non-linear
Improvement

The joy
At the thought
That she was saved by a nurse
Who listened to her instincts

Going against
The doctor's feeble deliberations
Sending Mum to *les urgences**
Without further considerations

The joy
Of knowing that Mum and I would have
More time together after all
If everything carried on getting better

From the RER station near her home
I left for Paris with a lighter heart
Than the alternative
Would have allowed ...

And so I regretfully stand up
Gather my coat, scarf and suitcase
Let my face enjoy a few more sunny rays
And start walking out of my bewitching bubble

I give a coin to the guitar man
Beam my biggest smile and thank him
'C'était magnifique'
'Ah oui? Merci!'

The simplest of exchanges
Honey for our souls

---

* A&E in France

I leave the beautiful sounds and light of Les Halles
With a wound in my heart

I will remember my time here for ever
My time in no woman's land
Suspended between two lives
For a very brief hour

And I find myself on the Eurostar again …

Under the Channel again …

It feels like the time and space
In between my two countries
In between my two families
Is the only time I am ME

Unencumbered by memories
By language
By other people
By personae I present to the world

Which are not my pure soul

FIRST OUTING

It was unexpected
Even though, looking back
I had actually pictured it all
In my mind

Had dreamt about it
Maybe even had prayed for it

Mum was getting better
Finally out of the woods

It was time to check for sure

An X-ray confirmed it
She got the all-clear from her surgeon
Only to come out of his office
And find the ambulance staff

Gone

They would only
Come back
To pick her up
At 7pm!

It was lunch time
Three hours before my Eurostar
We could perhaps
Finally have some fun?!

I didn't give her time to think
Or the opportunity to decide
I was convinced we could do it

Only a few metres across from the hospital
Was the bistrot Le Saint Marcel

Mum sat in a wheelchair
Me so proud to push her
We reached it with ease

And took up our space
On the sunny terrace

I was looking forward to seeing Paris in the sunshine again
Paris in early spring, just me and my birthplace
But the Universe heard my plea for an outing in the sun
For my mum first and foremost

It seems it takes my 'orders' in turn
And then gets them all jumbled up

First I had asked for an outing with Mum
In the sun, in her wheelchair
At her physio clinic

But that didn't happen

Then I had asked for a lovely walk
By myself in Paris
And a heartfelt poem about it – just like last time

But that didn't happen either

That day, for some reason, there was a backlog

The Universe only granted me time with Mum
In her wheelchair
In the sun

– with the added bonus of *lunch* in the sun
It has to be said –

I remember, now
I *had* also requested that for myself!

The Universe gets confused sometimes
Gets orders muddled up

Or maybe it doesn't at all
It knows exactly
What you and others need
And how and where

I think Mum needed that, that day
Her first outing in nearly four months
The Parisian sun on her cheeks
The city sounds in her ears

And a lovely omelette in her tummy

It was the start of a new beginning
We could finally trust
That this story
Would end well

Bistrot

MAMAN AND MAMIE

I see Mamie in your eyes
I see Mamie in your cheeks
I hear Mamie in your voice
I hear Mamie in your wit

Your muscles have melted
Your fingers are thin and frail
Your forearms the size of my wrists
Your legs like a tree's fragile branches

Unstable on your dainty feet
Bent over your walking frame
You have suddenly become a version of Mamie
Who left us many moons ago

No matter
Your eyes are vibrant like hers
Deep and intelligent
And your mind as sharp as ever

Your astuteness
Anchored into your spirit
Your perseverance
Established in your heart

You always said you were more like your dad
But you are, in fact, just like your mum
Vivacious, clever, quick-witted
A force of nature, so determined to win in life

The recent chain of events happened
In order to show you precisely this
And to renew your zest for not just sheer existence
But for *thriving*

Death knocked on your door
Several times
These past four months
You said, 'Nope, I'm nowhere near ready'

You affirmed, 'I'm not done with life'
And thank goodness – for we have so much more
To talk about and experience
You and I!

BRITISH AND FRENCH THINGS

She wants British things
Crumpets and custard creams
Christmas pudding and brandy butter
Foamy shower gels and soft body unguents

I want French things
Cigarettes russes
Langues de chat
Le Petit Marseillais soap

To remind me of my childhood
To remember smells and flavours
Textures and consistencies
Of my very French past

When I am in her bathroom
I make sure to use her French supplies
– not her English ones
So as not to waste them on my now very British skin

Waitrose versus Carrefour
English recipes against French ones
We swap and discuss
All things British and all things French

Nearly thirty years in my adopted country
And still, nothing gets old for me
Or for her
We still marvel at everything British and French

LONELINESS

Nestled between the river Seine and the woods
Is my childhood home
Full of emptiness and loneliness
Empty, lonely

I filled my life with studies, food, friends, work
Yet it was still empty, still lonely
A mirror of my childhood home

For many years I was scared of discovering who I might be
At the bottom of the well, the empty well
Scared of discovering who I might not be
At the bottom of the well, the empty well

What if there was nothing there?
What if there was no one there?
What if I was nothing?
What if I was no one?

What if I was empty?
What if I had no substance?
What if I was inconsequential?
I never wanted to find out

So I filled myself up with food
And thoughts
And work
And busyness

Maybe I could disappear completely
Underneath all the things I put
In my body and mind
Maybe I could hide and never find out

But today …

I choose differently today
I choose to fill myself up with light and air
And beautiful thoughts
Or no thoughts at all

I choose differently today
I choose to be with *me*
I'm not scared of
Who I might be any more

I am willing to meet
Me
The pure me

I *want* to meet
Me
The real me

The one that is underneath all the layers
Of lies, worthless truths, emptiness and neglect

Mum's operations and swaying
Between life and death
And death and life
Has been a whole death-and-rebirth process

For us both

This is what we needed for ourselves
But also for the previous generations
And the next generations

A healing process
Where we got stripped bare
And started over

Fontaine Saint-Michel

WHAT'S IN A NAME

Always having to explain
Where my first name comes from
Is frustrating and exhausting

'But it's so pretty!'
'But it's so original!'
'But it's so interesting!'

But I'm so tired
Of revealing
Its origins

Still, I will do it here …

It is Corsican
It sounds Italian
Rather than French

Because Corsica
Was Italian
For centuries

Yet even in Corsica
The name is not that common
Let alone in France, let alone in England …

It means 'new home'
How fitting –
I have moved so many times in my life!

My first big move was to Paris
My second
To Nottinghamshire

Then to Warwickshire
Oxfordshire
Wiltshire

And a few times within each county …

Perhaps it is why, then
I can't be happy
With this first name

Wanting to 'move' it
Wishing I could change it
Willing it to go away

Yet …

Hearing it on the phone
Listening to my family
Say it with a French lilt

Seeing it written in our virtual group
So many times a day, a week, a month

I'm slowly getting used to it again

It is nearly pleasant
To see its letters
And hear its sounds

Still …

After a three-year identity crisis
Changing names several times
Unable to decide

This new, deeper crisis with Mum
And the publication of these poems
Are helping me reach a conclusion

I choose 'Laetitia'

My very French
Middle
Name

Laetus
Means 'joyful' in Latin
So even in these uncertain days

This is
What
I settle on

BACK HOME

And just like that, we're both
'Back home'
Together
As if nothing has happened

It lasted exactly five months
A whole initiation
Around death and rebirth
Both only metaphorical, thankfully

I put away the food shop
She prepares lunch
And we break bread together
Our favourite baguette

Just like in the good old times
As if nothing has happened

Everything and everyone in their place
Me in my childhood bedroom
Mum in her own bed near her own bathroom
Everything and everyone back to normal

Except once again
Just like post-pandemic
It's a *new* normal
We're both changed

There is a tiny bit of anxiety
In my heart
Anticipating wobbles and trips in all her moves
Just as for a toddler learning to walk

But within a few days
As she gains confidence
Walking around her home
So do I – in her strength, skills and determination

All is well
As if nothing has happened

There are still months of physio ahead
But Mum is as independent as ever
In her home
As if nothing has happened

However, we will never forget

SAINT-MALO AND VANNES

My tenth trip
In ten months
Looks wildly different
From all the others

After a time
To commiserate
The hour has come
To celebrate

Our closest friends and family members
Are all assembled
In our village hall
To honour Mum's recovery

To thank them for their unwavering support
Their kind words
Their love
And their friendship

Good food
Good mood
Good wine
Laughter and smiles

Then it is time
For our great adventure
In Brittany –
A seven-day road trip!

Who would have thought?
Nine months before
This was but a dream
A grand idea …

Sharing the driving
And conversations
We slowly approach
The mythical town of Saint-Malo

Home of the corsairs
Who brought wealth
From countries
Near and far

Her high walls protecting her
From the sea
And in times gone by
From pirates

Saint-Malo was my first taste of Bretagne
Her cobbled streets
Welcoming shops
And local delicacies

Crêpes, galettes and cider
Far breton, kouign-amann and lobster
It is a feast for our tastebuds
In the rain and the wind

Mum can't walk far or fast
But the car takes us to
As many places
As we can visit

To the old imposing houses
Along the coastline
To the port
And the castle

To sea views
Lighthouses
Statues
And towers

One afternoon I walk
Around the town
Alone on the ramparts
Near the sand and the sea

I meet Jacques Cartier and Robert Surcouf
And sip hot cocoa
With a view of sea and sky
Melting into each other

As they say in Brittany, it's always good weather
Whether it rains or shines …
I become accustomed to this grey view
And enjoy my time near the port

Off to other northern Britton towns we go
Then straight down to Vannes
To see my cousin
And his new life

Where the sun rays
Finally pierce the clouds –
It doesn't matter what they say
I still prefer *actual* good weather!

Vannes
Another walled town
Old timbered houses
Colourful walls

White sandy beaches
And grand abodes
I could stay here for ever
But home beckons once more

Mum is safe
Mum is happy
Mum is healthy
Mum is jolly

My trips will now be

More

Spaced

Out

NOVEMBER

The seventeenth of November
My mum would finally enter
The operating theatre
– the day I met a publisher

Lorna's her name, eyes of ember
An editor and proud owner
Of a shop in Cirencester
The day my life changed for ever

Bright books by many an author
Art prints in many a colour
My friend and I *had* to enter
And we took a little wander

Candles, paper and calendar
Lorna behind her computer
Greeted us with a smile bigger
Than a young child's in December

As if we were on Jupiter
Wide-eyed, in our hearts a flutter
We asked many questions of her
We had a fabulous banter

Owner, designer and publisher
She regaled us with tales brighter
Than lights on the Eiffel Tower
– enchanted by our encounter

Did not say I was a writer
Only talked about my daughter
Artist blooming like a flower
She also writes for her career

We could all have talked for ever
In the little shop of wonder
We bought a few books, no barrier
Said our 'byes but would remember

At home, it hit me like thunder –
Forgot to say I'm a writer!
A few months and poems later
Would send Lorna an e-letter

Wondered if she would consider
Reading poems about my mother
Pretty Paris and its river
– would she become my publisher?

You've read them, you know the answer!

I didn't know it'd be my mother
That would trigger and inspire
Many poems in my centre
And would lead me, torn asunder

Out of a deep well of horror
And turn me into an author
A locally published writer
Of hopefully a bestseller

BELONGING EVERYWHERE

I find myself in a bubble tea café in the town of my youth
I watch passers-by and remember my times here
So many hours spent in the centre
During my secondary-school years

I wonder what my old friends would look like now
By how much they have aged …
Would I recognise them?
Same faces but with wrinkles and a few greys?
Is this how they would describe me too?

How many more years will I come back to this town?
I never belonged here
I never belonged in my village
I hardly ever belonged in my parents' house

I still don't

A stranger everywhere I am
A stranger everywhere I go
Always a stranger

Yet also a woman of the world
Belonging everywhere

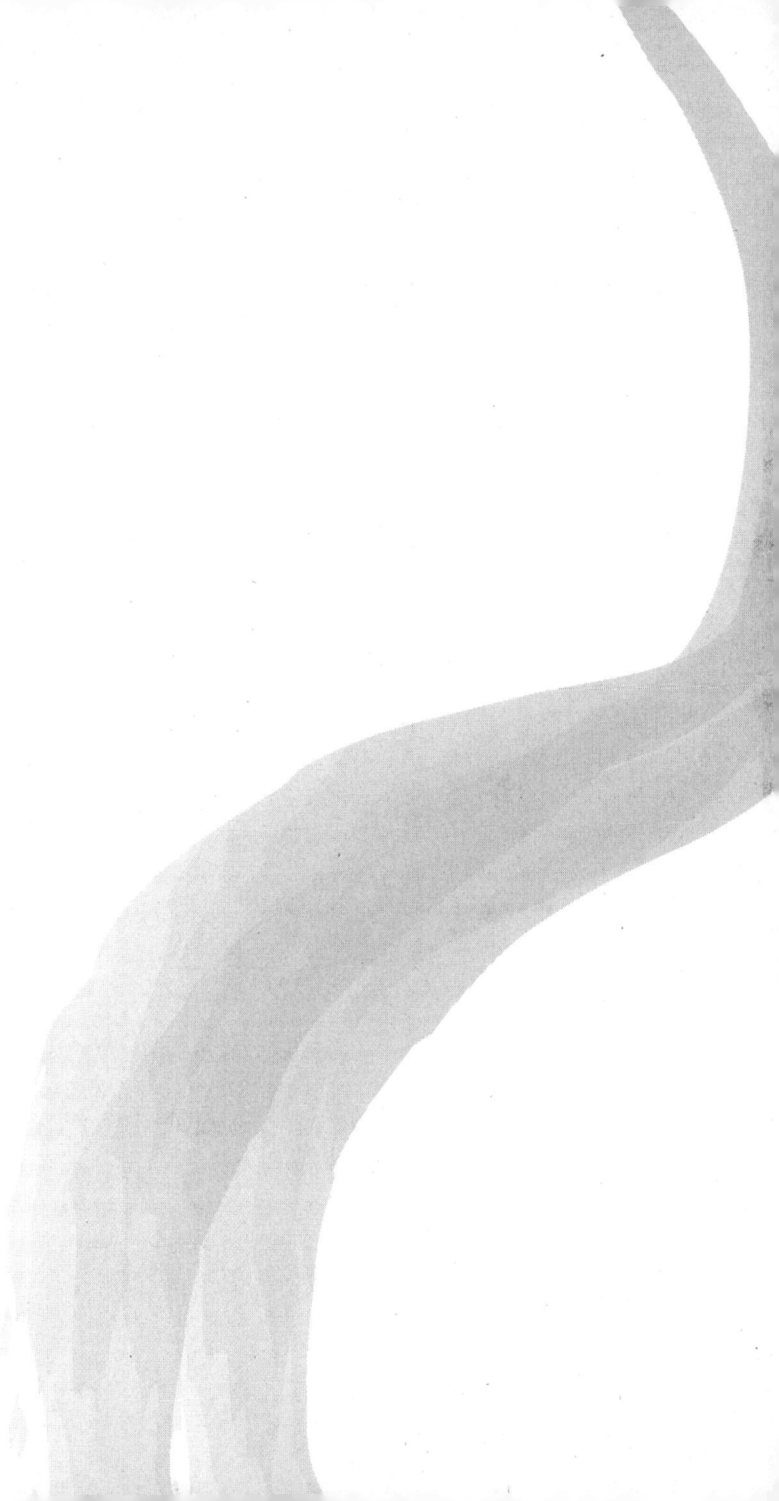

If you loved this book,
please leave a review ...

The best place to leave a review is on Waterstones.com or on Amazon

Reviews make our authors happy and help us to share news of their work with more readers. Thank you for your support!

Did you know that this book has been ethically printed in the UK on FSC certified paper made from a mixture of fibre from responsibly managed woodlands and recycled material?

Crumps Barn Studio
crumpsbarnstudio.co.uk

ACKNOWLEDGEMENTS

All my heartfelt and deep thanks to …
(in chronological order – no competition!)

Mum
It makes me sad that you had to go through
Such an awful time for so many months
In order for me to finally write and publish a book
But we can't choose what creativity decides
Or what serendipity puts on our path
It was such an honour
To be by your side
All those weeks
And as you know it was sweet as well as bitter
Bittersweet
Doux-amer
Ma douce mère

Mamie
My dear grandma
I wish you were still here
So I could ask you all the questions I have
About writing, history and your life
It was so rich
Thank you for leaving behind a legacy of
Words, stories and memoirs
For myself and my children
I hope to do the same –

This is only book number 1!
Thank you for being there when I shared
The first few pages of one of my novels
At age 14!
I miss you

Tuti
You and I
Twelve years old
Each on a mattress
Writing our poems and stories
Such enduring memories!
Thank you for your presence
Through nearly four decades
And beyond the oceans
More recently
Thank you for introducing me to Goodreads
Allowing me to be closer to your reading encounters –
May books and writing always unite us!

Caro
Always making memories
In France *and* in England
Sharing experiences
Gifting each other meaningful books
Throughout the last 33 years
Through pregnancies and motherhood
Through thick and thin
Always your wonderful advice
Thank you, dear friend

Anne-Laure and Gwen
Born on the same day
Of the same year
It was meant to be
My lovely twin friends
I'll always cherish our year in Paris
Our friendship remains wonderful and strong
Despite the distance
Thank goodness for WhatsApp groups!

Babs
I would never have guessed
That our chance encounter in 1995
Would lead to such a deep friendship
Without you
I wouldn't have studied in England
I wouldn't have written books in English
This poetry collection wouldn't have been born …
Travel, books, writing, photos (enlarged and framed!)
We have shared so many passions
In the last three decades
Thank you for your eagle eyes
For your writing and design support
For being by my side in Paris
In the early days of Mum's ordeal
And for witnessing the first drafts
Of the first few poems that were written
Around that time
The poem 'Nine years' in this collection
Is dedicated to you, of course!

Teresa
You gave me my first freelance editor job
I will never forget how I felt
When I first met you
Such surprise
Such elation!
I expected a middle-aged woman
You were about my age!
My editor, my bridesmaid, my friend
Our children now good chums too
How special is our story
In my adopted country

Agnès, Helen and Kim
The perfect trio
These past 22 years
It's not a Catch 22
It's not *22 v'là les flics!*
It's pure joy to meet up with you
Throughout the years
And many counties –
Out of my one-year parenthesis at 'you know where'
Was born our lovely forever friendship

Christelle and Valérie
Thank you for your omnipresence
During those hard months
Your messages and your calls
Your unwavering support
Having two French friends who understood

Made the experience just about bearable
Here's to many more wild swims
And shopping sprees!

Leigh
I will always cherish our chats
In the office
Around the village
Via email and messages
Editing, proofreading, managing
Freelancing, reading and writing
Words, books and stories are our world
In all the languages we speak!
Thank you for your unwavering support
And for your early reading of some of these poems

Kamilya
From hypnobirthing to writing –
Who would have thought, back in 2012!
Moving closer to you has been a blessing
It has been so lovely to connect with you
Over so many topics
But most of all
You have been part
Of this whole poetry journey
Since day 1
During that chance encounter
In November 2023 in Cirencester
On the day of Mum's first operation –
There are no coincidences!

Lee
Thank you for holding the fort
And taxiing me to and from Swindon station
In my absence, you rose to the challenge
Of working and looking after the children and the house
With the added bonus of supporting me emotionally and practically
My phone calls in tears from Paris
My messages of hope
You went along with it all
The ups and the downs
The fears and the reassurances
My Rock, thank you
I love you

Lux and Ceya
These harrowing months have turned you into
Resilient and self-reliant young people
I am SO proud of you
Thank you for your presence in my world
You mean everything to me
Thank you for your wisdom around the design
And the words of some of these poems
I sincerely hope we can all write a book together one day!
Ceya, a big thank-you for your beautiful illustrations
They really bring the poems to life

And finally Lorna
My publisher, editor, formatter
And cover designer extraordinaire

Thank you for believing in me
And giving me
This opportunity
Working with you has been such a joy
Your editing and design flair are without equal
'November' is dedicated to you
And our lovely encounter in a tiny street
Of Cirencester
That day, I never thought a book of my own
Would come out of it!

All my thanks, too, to my good friends Amanda, Carole, Catherine C, Céline, Debbie, Isabelle R, Jo, Kathy, Michael, Rhonda, Sacha and Tania, and to all my and my mum's friends and family who supported us, in particular Aude, Camilla, Catherine D, Catherine L, Cathy, Chantal, Christophe Mi, Christophe Mo, Claire D, Claire H, Claude, Dominique, Dothy, Elisabeth, Eric, Franceline, Franck, Gaëlle, Givrette, Hervé, Isabelle L, Jacques, Jacqueline, Jean-Claude, Jean-Luc, Jean-Paul, Jean-Pierre, Jocelyne, Joëlle, Justine, Luc, Manou, Marc-Antoine, Marion, Martine B, Martine M, Miquette, Monica, Monique, Nicole, Pam, Pascaline, Patrick, Robin, Serge, Steve, Susan, Virginie et Yvette.

Thank you again, WhatsApp groups!

Also in memory of Axelle, who left us during those months.

ABOUT THE AUTHOR

Laetitia Devic started writing when she was eight years old. Born in Paris, she has lived in the UK since 1995 and now lives in Wiltshire with her husband, two children and cat. An avid reader of literary fiction and memoirs, she never thought poems would come to her as her main form of writing. Creativity is full of surprises! *Between Two Lives / Entre Deux Vies* is her first poetry collection.

Follow her on Instagram and Facebook:

@laetitia.devic.author

Find out more about Laetitia and her writing at:

www.laetitiadevic.uk